A Communion Preparation Course for 7-11s

SHARE

See Hear Accept Receive Enjoy

NICK HARDING

kevin
mayhew

First published in 2002 by
KEVIN MAYHEW LTD
Buxhall, Stowmarket, Suffolk IP14 3BW
E-mail: info@kevinmayhewltd.com

9 8 7 6 5 4 3 2 1 0

ISBN 1 84003 927 2
Catalogue number 1500519

Cover design by Angela Selfe
Edited and typeset by Elisabeth Bates
Printed in Great Britain

Contents

About the author

Nick Harding grew up in Birmingham where he learned about Christianity from an early age. After going through the education system he taught in Nottinghamshire and has worked with a number of Christian organisations in a variety of roles ever since. As well as being a trustee of Scripture Union, occasionally working on radio and speaking at events and conferences, Nick also writes articles for a number of magazines and has written many books for and about working with children. He works as Children's Mission Support Officer for Southwell Diocese, supporting rural and urban churches in their work. Nick is a fan of the music of Elton John and Elgar, enjoys working out at the gym and walking in Sherwood Forest, and shares his life with his wife Clare, and sons Jared and Callum.

See . . .
God's work. Creation, the world, and us

Hear . . .
God's word. The fun, facts and framework for life

Accept . . .
God's way. Love, friendship, relationship and forgiveness

Receive . . .
God's meal. Bread and wine to remember Jesus

Enjoy . . .
God's future. Celebrating our life with God

How to use this course

This is a short Communion Preparation Course for children who are ready to learn more about Communion but are not at the stage of Confirmation. This course consists of five sessions in preparation for the first Communion, plus session outlines for two Parent Sessions and suggestions for the first Communion Service. By the end of the course those who take part in SHARE will have a good grounding in the basics of the Christian faith, the Bible and the true, powerful significance of Holy Communion.

Each of the five sessions has plenty of material to choose from depending on the facilities available and the size and nature of the group. The course provides more material than you need to use, giving you the flexibility to choose from the range of activities offered.

Sample letter and forms

The sample letter and forms are designed to be used before the course begins and during the course to invite others to the children's first Communion. They will need to be adapted to the individual situation, but give all the necessary basic information. These can be found at the back of the book.

Games

Each session has a number of games both for the whole group to do and for a few volunteers to take part in.

Bible

The course has readings and Bible stories suggested, with some drama and dramatic readings.

Activities

The activities range from craft ideas to written work, questionnaires, actions and thinking time.

Prayers

There are plenty of practical prayer suggestions, responses and planned prayers to use.

Resources

Where specific items are required for each activity this is made clear by the arrow icon (➜). In most cases the equipment or resources will be easily available and require little preparation time.

And there's more . . .

There are some simple activities suggested for the children to complete between sessions.

All the worksheets are at the back of the book.

Practical points

The course is designed for 7-11 year olds, but is adaptable for other age groups and ability ranges.

At least two leaders should always be present in order to conform to standard child safety guidelines.

Most of the activities do not require much space, and the more active games could take place outside if there is suitable space.

The course consists of five distinct sessions, although it could take place over a weekend or over ten shorter periods of time.

Each session contains up to 3 hours of activities. It is anticipated that users will select activities which will work best with the children concerned, and which provide a balance of activity, discussion and teaching.

Refreshments such as cola and biscuits or sweets, should be served at a mid-point during each session.

Children should be encouraged to attend church as well as attending the course. Attendance cards or stickers could be used as an incentive.

Introduction

For a number of years churches have been becoming more aware of the issues surrounding children in church, and in particular their exclusion from Holy Communion. In the Church of England it was the norm for young people to receive Communion only after Confirmation, while in other churches and denominations full participation in this rite by receiving Communion was a sign of church membership and may have followed 'adult' Baptism. Now things have changed, and many churches are encouraging young people to receive Communion at an earlier age, leaving church membership, adult Baptism or Confirmation until later teenage when they are more able to fully understand and accept the consequences of their decision.

This course is designed to help children aged 7-11 learn more about the Christian faith and the significance of Holy Communion as part of faith and worship. This course is short, active, and full of practical ideas for group leaders to use. It is not a Confirmation or Adult Baptism Course, and assumes that young people who so choose will have the option of following through their personal commitment at an older age. In addition the parents or guardians of the children should not be ignored, and to that end there are two session outlines to help them.

Receiving Communion is one of the many stages on the journey into faith, not the end of that journey. Through this course the children will have a grounding in the basics of Christianity, and will be better able to understand what it is they do as they take bread and wine. They should also have some of the knowledge they will need to make personal, meaningful decisions to continue following Christ when the time comes.

See . . .

God's work. Creation, the world and us

Introduction

We can only be aware of the awesomeness and majesty of God if we begin by thinking about his creation. We can see it all about us, in all that the world has to offer, and even in the mirror. As we see the hand of God at work in so many ways we begin to understand the power of God, and the power of his love for us.

Silent activity

Close your eyes and look into your own mind. You may see darkness, flashing lights, or you may see scenes of things that have happened to you over the last few days. We are going to look into that darkness silently for one minute.

Prayer

Learn the response: **Be with us now and give us your help.**

Father God, thank you that we are here.
Be with us now and give us your help.
Father God, thank you that we can see your work in creation.
Be with us now and give us your help.
Father God, thank you that we can see your work in each other.
Be with us now and give us your help.
Father God, thank you that we can find out more about you.
Be with us now and give us your help.

Game: I'm . . .

Sit the group in a circle and begin with one child describing themselves by saying 'My name is *N* and I'm blond/happy/tall/quiet, etc'. Then the next person begins by going back to the first person and saying 'Her name is *N* and she is . . ., and my name is *P* and I'm . . .', and so on. The last person in the circle therefore has to remember all the other names and how each person described themselves.

Badges

➜ *Sticky paper labels, pencils and crayons*
Give each member of the group a large sticky label, and ask them to write

their names on them. They should then draw on the label a few things that they are into or enjoy doing. Once they have all finished they should move around the room looking at each others' 'badges' and asking questions about the things they have drawn.

Talk: Creation

Ask the children the question 'If God made everything, who made God?' There are plenty of things about God that we will never understand, and the answer to this question is one of them. Christians believe that it all had to begin somewhere, and it all began with God. God created the world, whether that happened in six actual days of 24 hours in each, or over six periods of time.

The beginning

Ask the group to close their eyes. As they imagine darkness and silence slowly read out Genesis 1:1-5. Invite the group to try to picture the movement of the Spirit of God across the waters, and then read it out again.

Creation search

→ *Paper, pencils and crayons, Bibles*

Give each child a piece of A4 paper, which they should fold to form 6 boxes on the paper. Then in pairs give them Bibles, and ask them to fill each box with drawings and words to describe the six days of creation from Genesis 1. If time allows they should colour in their pictures.

Active animals

Invite the children to noisily and actively act out the creature from God's creation that you name. You should choose a range of animals from noisy ones (ape, lion, elephant) to quieter or smaller ones (slug, mouse, tortoise).

Male and female

Ask a boy and a girl to come out and stand at the front. Explain that God decided to make us as we are, with boys being different from girls and men different from women. Then read out the accounts of the creation of man and woman – Genesis 1:26 and Genesis 2:18-24.

Pictures and names

→ *Pictures of leaders as babies, baby-name books*

Introduce this activity by explaining that we can see God's creation in each of us. We may have seen pictures of ourselves as a baby (show your baby pictures) and been told how special we were and looked when we were born. As we see people, including the others in this group, we can see God's work.

Give out the baby-name books (available from libraries, free with parenting magazines, and from any young couple expecting a baby). Ask the children to find their own name and learn what it means. Then ask them to tell the others what they have found out.

Blindfold identity
➜ *A blindfold*
Invite one child to come to the front of the group, blindfold them, and then explain that another child will also come to the front and sit in front of them. The blindfolded child must identify who the other one is by means of touch.

Fact file: Me
➜ *'Fact file' sheet, pencils and crayons*
Give out the 'Fact file' sheet and ask the group to fill it in honestly about themselves, including a self-portrait. If there is not enough time this could be completed at home.

We see God's work . . .
Learn the following phrase, saying it together:

We see God's work in the world he made.
We see God's work in the people he made.

Then devise some simple actions to use as you say this phrase, and practise them together.

Prayer
Father God, thank you that we have been here.
Be with us now and give us your help.
Father God, thank you that we can see your work in creation.
Be with us now and give us your help.
Father God, thank you that we can see your work in each other.
Be with us now and give us your help.
Father God, thank you that we have found out more about you.
Be with us now and give us your help.
Father God, be with us as we go from here.
Be with us now and give us your help.

And there's more . . .

Ask the children to write down how their parents and others answer the following two questions:

- What is good about God's world?
- How would you describe me? (name of each child)

Hear . . . 3
God's word. The fun, facts and framework for life

Introduction

After seeing the work of God we now think about hearing the word of God. The word of God as given to us through the Bible is not only a book full of stories. The Bible contains the guidelines for life, offering us a framework within which to live. It also gives us the model for Holy Communion itself.

Silence

Ask the group to sit quietly and listen to any sounds they can hear. They should sit and listen for at least one minute.

Listen about the world

Remind the group of last time's 'And there's more' activity that they should have done at home. Then get those who feel able to read out the things the adults they asked said about them.

'Listen about me' prayers

Each person in the group should in turn read out some of the things others said about them. This should be done in a prayerful atmosphere, with the following line after each person:
Thank you, God, for . . . Thank you that you love him/her.

Sounds around

Everyone in the group should stand in a circle. Ask each person in the circle to say one sound they hear at home, at school or at church, and then sit down. Once everyone is sitting, go around again, this time with everyone standing in turn, and so on.

Reading aloud
➜ *Bible*

Read Psalm 119:105-112 to the group from a suitable version of the Bible (Good News or Contemporary English Version). Then read it again, the second time making deliberate mistakes as you go along. Ask the children to spot the deliberate mistakes and tell you what you should have said.

Talk: Word, commands and law

Remind the group that the reading is about the word of God, what we now call the Bible. The writer uses different words for the same thing, and all the words we could use too. God asks us to hear his word and put what he says into action in our lives by living the right way and doing what his word says. The word of God that we should listen to is like a light which makes the right way clear for us.

Talk: Blockbusting Bible

➜ *A Bible story on video (e.g. The Prince of Egypt, The Miracle Maker), video player and screen*

Show a clip lasting about 5 minutes of a film based on the Bible. Remind the children that there have been more films made about the Bible than any other subject. Parts of the Bible have been translated into over 300 languages, and there are at least 30 versions in English available to buy. The Bible sells more copies than any other book every year – it is always the best of the best-sellers. Over a million copies of the Bible are sold in the UK every year.

Interesting Bible chunks

The group should stand in a circle with plenty of space around them. Go around the circle naming them in turn: LAW, HISTORY, PROPHECY, SONGS, GOSPELS, EPISTLES. Then read out the following passage, explaining that every time they hear their 'name' mentioned they must leave the circle and run around the outside in a clockwise direction, back to their place.

The word Bible means a collection of books, a bit like a library. There are 66 books in the Bible. It has all sorts of writing in it, with SONGS and stories, letters called EPISTLES, and GOSPELS which are books that tell the Good News about Jesus. The Old Testament, the books written before Jesus, have lots of LAW and HISTORY books, and PROPHECY books written by God's messengers about what God would do in the future. There are Psalms or SONGS, written at different times in HISTORY. The New Testament has the GOSPELS, the stories of Jesus. It also has letters written to believers in the first churches called EPISTLES. With EPISTLES and GOSPELS there are also books about what happened when churches began. So, with the LAW, HISTORY and PROPHECY books as well as SONGS, EPISTLES and GOSPELS there is plenty of interest to be found in the Bible.

Best Bible bit

➜ *'Best Bible bit' sheet, pencils, Bibles*

Begin with the children talking with you about what stories and parts of the Bible they like best. Then hand out the sheets and ask them to have a go at writing the story, writing why it is a favourite Bible bit for them, and drawing a picture to go with it.

Stop and listen

➜ *Bible*

Read or tell the Bible story of Samuel and Eli from 1 Samuel 3:1-10. Explain the following points:

- Samuel was busy rushing around for Eli, and didn't at first hear that it was God speaking to him.
- Samuel had to learn to stop and listen in order to hear what God had to say to him.
- Samuel listened to God, and became a great Prophet (messenger) and leader because he listened to God.

Long laws

➜ *Paper, Bibles, pencils*

Explain that parts of the Bible were written to give people guidelines about how to live. Some of those rules and laws were for that time, but don't make sense now. But all Christians try to follow 10 rules that God gave for everyone.

Ask everyone to look up the Ten Commandments from Exodus 20:1-17. In small groups or pairs they should first of all write down the Ten Commandments which God gave. Then they should try to write them in a more modern language. During this activity they may need help to understand some of the meanings of the laws, and you will need to be sensitive when dealing with 'adultery'.

Bible notes

➜ *Copies of Bible notes for children (Scripture Union 'Snapshots' notes or CWR 'Topz' notes), Bibles, pencils*

Give each child a copy of the notes and ask whether they have seen or used them before. Then get all the group to turn to the current day's notes and work through the suggestions given. At the end explain that we can sometimes find it hard to hear what the Bible has to say to us because it is not always easy. These notes are written to help everyone hear more from God and his word.

Exciting Bible
➜ *Simple costumes*
Involve all the children in groups, each group preparing and acting out one of the following stories. Every story is an exciting story from the Bible, proving that it has the best adventures of any book ever!
David defeats Goliath – 1 Samuel 17:41-54.
Moses crosses the Red Sea – Exodus 14.
Jesus feeds 5000 – John 6:1-14.

Bible quiz
Have sweets or other small prizes available to give one to every child who gets an answer right. Use the following questions or any others based on the Bible activities this session.

• How many international translations?	300
• How many English versions?	30
• What is an Epistle?	Letter
• How many books in the Bible?	66
• What do the Gospels tell us about?	Jesus
• What are Prophecy books?	The future
• Where are the Psalms or songs – Old or New Testament?	Old
• Name two Commandments	
• What was Goliath?	Giant

Hearing you
➜ *A CD player and quiet worship songs playing*
For this prayer time teach this response:
Thank you for hearing us, help me to hear you.

Thank you, Father God,
that you gave your word to your people throughout history.
Thank you for hearing us, help me to hear you.
Thank you, Father God,
that you gave law, history, letters, gospels and prophecy to help us.
Thank you for hearing us, help me to hear you.
Thank you, Father God,
that your word is still worth hearing, understanding and following.
Thank you for hearing us, help me to hear you.
Help me, Father God,
to always hear what you have to say to me, and to always do what you say.
Thank you for hearing us, help me to hear you.

And there's more

Allow the group to take home their copies of Bible notes used earlier (e.g. Snapshots or Topz) and ask them to do the reading and activities every day until the next session. They should bring the notes back with them.

Accept . . .
God's way. Love, friendship and forgiveness

Introduction
The Christian journey is about acceptance. God accepts us as we are, even though we make mistakes. In return we accept the friendship and love of Jesus, and his forgiveness when we are truly sorry for going wrong. When we accept God in our lives we are moving towards a deeper relationship with him.

See and Hear
➜ *Inflated balloons*

Split the group into two teams, and ask them questions about the last two sessions, 'See' and 'Hear'. You could use some of the questions from the 'Hear' quiz, or make up your own questions. Each time a group answers a question correctly give them a balloon. The group with the most balloons at the end of the quiz wins, and can burst all the balloons!

Prayer
Learn the response: **Be with us now and give us your help.**

Father God, thank you that we are here.
Be with us now and give us your help.
Father God, thank you that we can see your work in creation.
Be with us now and give us your help.
Father God, thank you that we can see your work in our friends.
Be with us now and give us your help.
Father God, thank you that we can find out more about following you.
Be with us now and give us your help.

Bible notes
Ask the group how they got on with the Bible notes since the last session. Find out whether they learned anything from doing them, and whether they enjoyed the activities. Explain that to hear from God we need to get into the habit of listening to him.

My friends
➜ *A teddy bear*

Begin by talking about the teddy bear you have chosen. Tell the story of when it was bought, and who it belongs to. For young children dolls or teddy bears can be friends, and are treated as if they are real and living.

Sit the group in a circle and pass the teddy bear around. Each young person who holds it must say one thing about their friends. They should try to describe what makes a good friend, why they remain friends, and so on. Remind them from time to time that they are only allowed to speak while holding the teddy bear in order to give everyone a chance.

Wanted
→ *Wanted poster, pencils, crayons*
Give out the Wanted posters, and ask each child to fill one in about their best friend or friends. They should draw their friend, and write a few lines about what they are like and why they are friends. This can be taken home at the end of the session to be finished if time is limited.

Bible reading 1
→ *Bibles*
Ask two children to share the reading of Matthew 4:18-22. Then ask the group to suggest answers to these questions:

- Why did Jesus choose fishermen rather than professors or 'clever' people?
- Do you think even Jesus needed to have friends?
- Why did Jesus need other people to go with him, work with him and help him?
- Why did Simon, Andrew, James and John all leave what they were doing in order to follow Jesus?
- What was it about Jesus that drew people to him?

Following the leader
Find some space to play this traditional game. Begin by explaining that Jesus' friends, his disciples, followed him and helped him wherever he went. Then play 'Follow the leader', with each child in turn having a turn as the leader, leading the others in jumping, running, etc.

Bible reading 2
Before reading the Bible passage explain that Peter was one of Jesus' friends, and followed Jesus. But even he made mistakes and needed forgiveness.

Read out Matthew 26:69-75 once. Then read it again, pausing at random points during each verse for the children to suggest the next word.

Sorry sheet

➔ *Sorry sheet, pencils*

Explain that if Peter was filling in a Sorry sheet he would probably have written 'denying Jesus' on it. We can all be friends of Jesus, we can all follow him, and we can all say 'sorry' to Jesus and receive his forgiveness. Ask the young people to fill in their own Sorry sheet, listing things they know they do which they shouldn't, and so on. You may want to do a sheet too, and explain what it says to the group as an example.

Confession prayer

➔ *Candle, matches, bin, 'Confession prayer' copied for each child*

For this activity it would be good to go to the Altar or a side chapel in church, if that is possible. If not, set up a table with a candle on it in your room.

Place the bin in front of the table or altar, and hand out copies of the Confession prayer. After some time in quiet to think and read through the words of the prayer you should say the first part in unison:

There are things I do that I regret.
There are things I say that I wish I could take back.
There are things I think that I know are wrong.
There are things I don't do that I should.
All the things I ignore, all the things I do, all the things I say,
and all the things I think I give to you.

At this point the children should bring forward their Sorry sheet and place it in the bin as a sign that God receives us and forgives us when we are truly sorry. Once that is done, lead the children through the next prayer, with them saying the response:

We have a God who wants us to follow him.
Thank you, God, that we can follow you.
We have a God who sent his son to be our friend.
Thank you, Jesus, that we can be your friend.
We have a God who promises to forgive us.
Thank you, God, that you forgive us right now.
We have a God who will be with us always.
Thank you, God, that we can always know your love. Amen.

Bible reading 3

➔ *'Jesus and Peter' script for three children*

Ask the three children chosen beforehand to read out their parts of the script. It may help them if you highlight their lines in advance.

Narrator	After Jesus and the disciples had shared breakfast Jesus went to one side and said to Simon Peter:
Jesus	Simon, son of John, do you love me more than these others?
Simon Peter	Yes, Lord, you know that I love you.
Jesus	Take care of my lambs.
Narrator	Again, Jesus spoke to Simon.
Jesus	Simon, do you love me?
Simon Peter	Yes. You know that I love you!
Jesus	Take care of my sheep.
Narrator	A third time Jesus asked Simon the same question, by which time Peter was getting a little frustrated.
Simon Peter	Yes, Lord, you know that I love you. You know everything.

Accepting talk

This week we have thought about Acceptance. Jesus offered Peter his friendship, and he offers us his friendship too. For Peter and for us that friendship is not just for a day or week or year – it is for life. Jesus called Peter to follow him and accept his leadership. If we are true followers of Jesus we will try to do what is right all the time. Jesus also offered forgiveness even though Peter went wrong. We are offered that forgiveness too.

And there's more . . .

At home the children should complete their Wanted poster about friends.

'Major meals' sheet: Using the sheet the children should fill in things and draw their favourite meals in preparation for the next session.

Receive...
God's meal. Bread and wine to remember Jesus

Introduction
After accepting Jesus and the forgiveness that he offers we are more able to understand what we do when we receive the bread and wine. Food is important in the traditions of both the Jewish and Christian faiths, and as we prepare to take part in a special meal we learn about the significance of the meal we receive.

Major meals
➜ *'Major meals' sheets, stopwatch*
Ask for three volunteers to come out to the front. Then ask each one in turn to talk for 30 seconds about meals that they enjoy. If they hesitate for too long then they're out of the game. Make sure you have prizes for all those who are willing to have a go. Then ask any others to tell you what they put on their 'Major meals' sheets.

Food prayers
Sit the group in a circle. At appropriate points all of the group should say one thing they enjoy to eat for breakfast, lunch, and so on.

Thank you, God, for food. Thank you for the food I enjoy for breakfast. Thank you for ……………..

Thank you, God, for food. Thank you for the food I enjoy for lunch. Thank you for …………….

Thank you, God, for food. Thank you for the food I enjoy for main meals. Thank you for ………

Meals talk
Discuss how meals can be very special times. Talk about special meals at Christmas or Easter, about birthday meals, and about occasions when people go out to restaurants for meals. Meals are used to mark and celebrate special occasions, and sometimes to remember things that have happened in the past. The Passover meal in the Bible was used to remember the past, when God protected his people from death.

Meal people

→ *'Meal people' sheets, Bible*

Give out the 'Meal people' sheets. Explain that throughout the Bible meals are important as times when families and friends met together. Many important events in the Bible happened at meal times.

The young people should work on their own or in pairs to look up the meals mentioned on the sheet and write down who was at each meal. The correct answers are:

Genesis 3:6	Adam and Eve
Genesis 25:29-31	Jacob and Esau
Exodus 16:13-16	Moses, Aaron and the people
Daniel 5:1	King Belshazzar, 1000 men
John 6:5-9	Jesus, disciples, 5000 others
Luke 24:36-43	Jesus, disciples

Passover reading

→ *Story version of the Passover*

Read out a story account of the Passover, based on Exodus 11-14. Explain that God didn't want to hurt others, but they had defied him so much that there was no other choice. Point out that the Passover meal became very important to God's people, and all the foods meant something.

The mark of blood

→ *Large sheet of white paper, red paint or marker pen*

Explain that the mark of blood was put on the door posts to show God that they needed his help and support.

Put the paper on the wall, covering the wall behind it (and if using paint, the floor below also) and invite each child to think of one thing they need God's help with. Then in turn ask them to come out and make a mark on the sheet of paper to show God that they need his help. You may want to extend the activity by asking them to share the things they have asked God to help them with, if they want to.

Passover meal

→ *Parsley, bread, radish, honey, lamb bone, red wine, white tablecloth, candle and matches*

Place the cloth and candle on a table and light the candle. Then put each of the items on to the cloth one by one explaining what their significance is as you do so. These are not all the items used for a Passover feast, and the definitions given are simplified.

Parsley – nature and life. God gave us the world, and he gives life to us all.

Bread – the food eaten in Egypt, to remind the people of their suffering.

Radish – bitterness. Bitter taste to remind them of their slavery.

Honey – sweetness. Sweet hope that only God can give.

Lamb – sacrifice. Lambs were sacrificed to protect the people.

Red wine – celebration. Red wine to celebrate the laws and guidance of God.

Once you have described the significance of each item ask the children to taste them all. Encourage even the most reluctant ones to have a go in order to be part of the 'feast'.

Communion communication
➜ *Tape recorders (Dictaphones are best)*

In pairs or small groups ask the children to think about and discuss what Communion is, and what they have seen and understood about it. Then ask one of the pair or group to act as an interviewer and ask questions of the others about Communion. If time and situation allow, play back some of the responses to the whole group.

Receive this
➜ *Bible*

Ask the group to close their eyes and picture a group of followers of Jesus meeting together in a room and sharing the special meal together. Jesus' followers would be remembering their friend who had gone to heaven maybe only months before, while we are remembering what Jesus did for us by dying on the cross. Then read the account of Holy Communion from 1 Corinthians 11:23-26. After a time of quiet, explain to the young people that we base modern Communion services on this passage, and try to make it as close to what Jesus did as possible.

Taste
➜ *Communion wine and bread or wafers*

Most of the children will not be familiar with the taste of the bread or wafers used in your church, or the taste of the wine or juice commonly used. In order to prepare them for the service when they receive bread and wine for the first time it is wise to allow them to taste it in advance. The elements should not be blessed. If possible take them to the front of church and act out a little of what they should do to receive Communion. You may also want to practise holding the chalice and how much to drink, or when to drink from the small cups depending on your church tradition. Advise the children how to use wafers so that they do not stick to the roof of the mouth. This should be a practical, light-hearted activity in order that they are prepared for the 'real thing'.

'We receive' prayers

Teach the response: **We receive all this from you.**

Ask the children to sit quietly and lay their hands open on their laps as a sign of being open to God and willing to receive from him. Then read out the prayer, with the children joining in with the response.

You made the world, and you gave us life.
We receive all this from you.
You gave us your son, and you give us your forgiveness.
We receive all this from you.
You give us love, and you give us your hope.
We receive all this from you.
You give us bread and wine to remember Christ's death.
We receive all this from you.
You give us hope for our future, and a plan for our lives.
We receive all this from you.

And there's more . . .

At home the children should ask older friends and adults what they remember about the first time they received Communion. It would help if the children wrote down what they were told ready for the next session.

Enjoy . . .
God's future. Celebrating our life with God

Introduction
It is easy to see the first Communion, with all the preparation, as the end point of the process. But for all of us the journey of faith takes a lifetime, and there is so much more for us to experience and enjoy about our faith.

Prayer
Learn the response: **Be with us now and give us your help.**

Father God, thank you that we are here.
Be with us now and give us your help.
Father God, thank you that we can see your work in creation.
Be with us now and give us your help.
Father God, thank you that we can receive your love for us.
Be with us now and give us your help.
Father God, thank you that we can find out more
about our future with you.
Be with us now and give us your help.

First Communion memories
The young people should have asked parents and friends about their memories of their first Communion. Go around the group asking the children to share the things they have found out.

You enjoy . . .
Sit the group in a circle and ask one of the children to stand in the centre. That volunteer should then look around the group and name each person in turn, saying one thing about them and what they enjoy. Then another child takes the centre of the circle, and so on. You may want to get this activity going by being the first in the centre of the circle.

Needs for a journey
Stand all the group up, and explain that they are going to imagine that they are going on a journey. Then name the journey from the list below, and ask

the children to suggest items that will help them on that journey. Those who make a good suggestion should then sit down.

A holiday somewhere hot and sunny

A trek up a snow-covered mountain

The journey to school

A late-night walk in the countryside

A trip to London on the train

Finish by explaining that we are all on a journey through life, and there are some things that we need. Ask for suggestions which may include food, drink, clothes, God, Bible, Jesus, Holy Spirit, etc.

Journey of life

➡ *'Journey of life' sheet, pencils*

Give out the sheets, explaining that we are all on a journey and many things have happened to us all on our journey so far. Ask them to fill in the major events of their lives between birth and now, and also to continue filling in what they hope may happen in the future.

Once they have finished ask some of the children to talk the group through what they have put on their sheet.

The Road to Emmaus reading

➡ *Bible or story version of Luke 24:13-35*

Read out the Bible passage or story version, possibly with three children acting out the main parts as you read it.

Remind the group of the phrase from the passage 'Jesus himself walked with them'. This is what Jesus is willing to do for all of us for the rest of our lives. The journey of life, like the journey to find out more about God, goes on and Jesus wants to be with us all the way on that journey. With Jesus walking with us we can enjoy everything that happens in our life.

Flame hat

➡ *Strips of card, brightly coloured paper, paper clips, scissors, glue sticks*

The children should work in pairs. Each pair should take two strips of card and decorate them with flames cut from brightly coloured paper and stuck on to the strips. Once the strips are covered in flames they should help each other put them on their heads, using the paper clips to hold the 'hats' on.

Pentecost reading and talk

➡ *Bible or story version of Pentecost (Acts 2:1-6)*

Ask the group to wear their hats and then close their eyes, imagining the scene. Ask them to think what it would be like to be worried and feeling lonely after Jesus went back to heaven, and confused about who the 'helper' was that they were told to wait for. Then read out the account of the first Pentecost. After the reading explain to the children that once the Spirit came on the followers they were changed, and enjoyed being able to do so much more for God.

The Holy Spirit
→ *Bibles for the group to use in pairs, paper and pencils*
Give out a Bible, pencil and sheet of paper to pairs or threes. Ask each small group to look up the fruits of the Spirit in Galatians 5:22-23 and make a list of the things that the Holy Spirit gives us.

Ask the children to feed back what they discovered from the passage, and take each fruit of the Spirit in turn, leading discussion about what it means. Finish by explaining again that God is with us through his spirit, and therefore we should aim to show all the fruits of the Spirit ourselves.

Inviting the Spirit
→ *CD player and quiet worship song or music*
Play the quiet music in the background. Ask the children to close their eyes and think about their hopes for the future. Remind them that God wants to be with us throughout our lives, and offers us his Spirit to help us.

Invite the children to keep their eyes closed and open their hands on their laps in order to invite God to send his Spirit to help us for the future. Sit silently with the music playing for as long as is possible before the children become unsettled.

Closing prayer
Remind the children of the response used a few sessions ago:
Thank you for hearing us, help me to hear you.

Thank you, Father God,
that you gave your word to your people throughout history.
Thank you for hearing us, help me to hear you.
Thank you, Father God,
that you gave law, history, letters, gospels and prophecy to help us.
Thank you for hearing us, help me to hear you.
Thank you, Father God,
that your word is still worth hearing, understanding and following.
Thank you for hearing us, help me to hear you.

Thank you, Father God,
that you want to be with us for the rest of our lives,
and we can always enjoy knowing you.
Thank you for hearing us, help me to hear you.

Finish by reminding the group of the date of the rehearsal and the service.

Parent session 1:
See, Hear and Accept

Beginning

Open with a prayer or time of quiet, before going through the structure of the course being delivered to the children:

SEE . . . God's work. Creation, the world, and us.

HEAR . . . God's word. The fun, facts and framework for life.

ACCEPT . . . God's way. Love, friendship, relationship and forgiveness.

RECEIVE . . . God's meal. Bread and Wine to remember Jesus.

ENJOY . . . God's future. Celebrating our life with God.

Introductions

Ask the group to introduce themselves, and tell the group one thing about their child who is preparing for Communion, and one thing about themselves.

See . . .

1. Ask the group to close their eyes as you read Genesis 1:1-2. As you do so they should focus on the words and the scene of God's Spirit at work, creating the world and humankind.

2. Sit the group in a circle and invite them to speak of the signs of God's creation that appeal to them, be it the countryside, animals, etc. Remind them that their children are a sign of God's creation too and it is our role to protect them and lead them in the right paths.

Hear . . .

1. Discuss with the group one passage from the Bible which is special to you, and read it to them. Then ask them to talk about any passage that has special meaning for them.

2. Read out Psalm 119:105-112. Remind the group that the Bible contains the framework for our life and faith, and as well as encouraging the young people who are preparing for Communion to read the Bible, they, the parents, should also.

3. Look at Colossians 3:20-21. Invite the parents to discuss the challenges of these verses.

Accept...

1. Ask any parents who feel able to share about their own personal journey of faith from childhood to now. What do they think it means to receive God's love? Remind the parents that this first Communion is a step on the journey for their children.

2. Read out the parable of the prodigal son (Luke 15:11-32). In small groups or pairs ask the group to discuss how the father, prodigal son and elder son felt when a) the younger son left home, and b) the younger son came home.

3. Spend some time in quiet, reflecting on the forgiveness that God offers us. Use an appropriate Confession prayer, or simply enjoy the silence.

Ending

Remind the group of the date and time for their second session.

Parent session 2
Receive and Enjoy

Opening
Read out the following statements during a time of quiet:

We see God in creation, and in our children.
We hear God's word, and aim to live by what it says.
We accept God's love and forgiveness for us.

Introductions
Sit the group in a circle and ask them in turn to talk a little about things that have happened to them since the previous session. Ask them what things have reminded them of God's creation and God's love for them.

Receive
1. Ask the group what they remember of the first time they saw or received Holy Communion. What did they think about it? What did it mean to them? Have their thoughts and views changed?

2. Mention the importance of the Passover, reminding the group of the first Passover before the Exodus from Egypt.

3. Read out the Luke account of the Last Supper (Luke 22:14-23) and ask the group in pairs to talk to each other about their understanding of the significance of the bread and wine.

4. Discuss the service for their children's first Communion. Talk the parents through what will happen, and what it means.

Enjoy
1. Give out pieces of paper and invite the parents to write on the sheet what they hope for their child's future. These could include career choices, academic or other achievements, and spiritual growth.

2. Ask members of the group to share what they have written down, and open up discussion on the potential for spiritual growth in the children. Mention that it is the parents' responsibility to ensure that children grow in faith and learn more about God.

3. Read Luke 18:18-24. Ask the group to suggest what they think the passage means. Is it about being financially rich? Is it about getting personal priorities right?

4. Invite the group to sit quietly and pray for themselves and their children as they prepare for their first Communion. Remind them that we are all on a journey of faith, and God has so much more for us to enjoy.

Ending

Give out the necessary dates for the rehearsal and service.

First Communion Service

These suggestions may help in thinking through and putting together a service to recognise the SHARE Course participants and give them an opportunity to feature as part of the service. However, each church situation is different, so careful planning and selection of suggestions is essential.

Part of a normal service
It may be suitable to receive the children for their Communion as part of a normal church service, marking the journey with a few comments or some of the elements suggested later.

Special service
Some churches choose to have a special service to recognise the end of the SHARE Course and make it an occasion for plenty of friends and relatives to be present. This could be followed by a light meal or refreshments, especially if family and friends have travelled a distance to be there.

Prayers
Some of the traditional prayers used and authorised in some denominations are worth using, although it is still worth spending a little time explaining the more difficult words and concepts.

You may think it possible to ask a few of the children to prepare some prayers for use during the service, and lead the prayer time. This may be especially appropriate for the intercessions.

It is also worth using some of the following prayers from earlier in the course, adapted for the service.

Prayer
Learn the response: **Be with us now and give us your help.**

Father God, thank you that we are here.
Be with us now and give us your help.
Father God, thank you that we can see your work in creation.
Be with us now and give us your help.
Father God, thank you that we can see your work in each other.
Be with us now and give us your help.

Father God, thank you that we can find out more about you.
Be with us now and give us your help.

You made the world, and you gave us life.
We receive all this from you.
You gave us your Son, and you give us your forgiveness.
We receive all this from you.
You give us love, and you give us your hope.
We receive all this from you.
You give us bread and wine to remember Christ's death.
We receive all this from you.
You give us hope for our future, and a plan for our lives.
We receive all this from you.

Thank you, Father God,
that you gave your word to your people throughout history.
Thank you for hearing us, help me to hear you.
Thank you, Father God,
that you gave law, history, letters, gospels and prophecy to help us.
Thank you for hearing us, help me to hear you.
Thank you, Father God,
that your word is still worth hearing, understanding and following.
Thank you for hearing us, help me to hear you.
Help me, Father God,
to always hear what you have to say to me, and to always do what you say.
Thank you for hearing us, help me to hear you.

There are things I do that I regret.
There are things I say that I wish I could take back.
There are things I think that I know are wrong.
There are things I don't do that I should.
All the things I ignore, all the things I do,
all the things I say and all the things I think I give to you.

We have a God who wants us to follow him.
Thank you, God, that we can follow you.
We have a God who sent his Son to be our friend.
Thank you, Jesus, that we can be your friend.
We have a God who promises to forgive us.
Thank you, God, that you forgive us right now.
We have a God who will be with us always.
Thank you, God, that we can always know your love. Amen.

A few words . . .

Some children may be mature and confident enough to speak for a few minutes on why they have decided to do the SHARE Course and what they feel about Jesus and their personal faith. This is often better if done in interview form with the course leader asking the questions, and practised a little beforehand.

Receiving Communion

If possible, it is significant for the children who have followed the course to receive Communion all together, perhaps before other members of the congregation. You may also want to experiment with other ways of sharing the elements of bread and wine on this occasion. For instance, if your church tradition is to use small cups of wine try passing a chalice round, and if you usually kneel in a line at the altar rail try standing in a circle.

Children involvement

In essence this service belongs to the children who have been part of the SHARE Course, and therefore it is good to involve them as much as possible without adding burdens which increase nervousness! Welcoming people as they arrive, handing out books, doing the readings, leading prayers, sharing about their faith, talking about the SHARE Course, and playing musical instruments or singing are all possible ways in which the child involvement could be increased.

SHARE
COMMUNION PREPARATION COURSE

Child's name _____

Address _____

_____

Tel _____ E-mail address _____

Baptised as a child? Yes/No

If yes, where and when? _____

_____

Please return this form to:

SHARE
COMMUNION PREPARATION COURSE

Dear

As you know, it is the policy of the church to prepare children to receive Communion. This preparation takes the form of the SHARE Course, which has been written for this age group. It covers a number of Christian basics, and forms good foundation for each child's personal journey of faith.

The course consists of five sessions for the children. In addition there are two sessions for parents. The details are below:

'SHARE' COMMUNION PREPARATION COURSE

SEE . . .
God's work; the world around us and who we are.   *Children only*

HEAR . . .
God's word, and what it teaches.   *Children only*

ACCEPT . . .
God's way. Love, friendship, relationship and forgiveness.   *Children only*

RECEIVE . . .
God's meal of Bread and Wine to remember Jesus.   *Children and parents*

ENJOY . . .
God's future. Celebrating our life with God.   *Children and parents*

If you would like your child to take part in the SHARE Communion Preparation Course please fill in the attached form as soon as possible.

Yours in Him,

FACT FILE

Name

Age

Likes

Happy

Dislikes

Family

Friends

Bad habits

Abilities

Moods

TV/Books

Sad

Favourite food

Sports

Best Bible Bit

Sorry

Major Meals

Delicious Dish

Glorious Grub

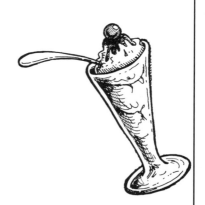

Yummy
Tummy-filler

Fantastic
Feasts